SURVIVORS
ON 9/11
Y SUSAN E. HAMEN
childsworld.com

ABOUT THE AUTHOR

Susan E. Hamen has written many books for young readers. She lives in Minnesota with her husband and two children. Like most Americans her age and older, she remembers exactly where she was on the morning of the 9/11 attacks. She had just gotten into her car to go to work. She turned on the radio and sat in disbelief at what she heard.

Published by The Child's World®
800-599-READ • www.childsworld.com

Photography Credits
Photographs ©: Mark Lennihan/AP Images, cover, 1; Don Halasy/Library of Congress, 5, 15; John Freidah - USA TODAY NETWORK, 6; Courtesy of the Prints and Photographs Division/Library of Congress, 8; Richard Drew/AP Images, 11; Carol M. Highsmith/Library of Congress, 12, 27; Larry Busacca/Getty Images for Time Warner/Getty Images Entertainment/Getty Images, 17; Mark Mainz/Getty Images Entertainment/Getty Images, 18; Michael Gordon/Shutterstock Images, 20; Shutterstock Images, 21; Paul Sancya/AP Images, 22; Aimee Malone/DVIDS, 24; Red Line Editorial, 26; Charlie Varley/varleypix.com, 28

ISBN Information
9781503889118 (Reinforced Library Binding)
9781503890893 (Portable Document Format)
9781503892132 (Online Multi-user eBook)
9781503893375 (Electronic Publication)

LCCN 2023950266

Printed in the United States of America

CONTENTS

FAST FACTS

- On September 11, 2001, **terrorists** attacked the United States. The terrorists **hijacked** four airplanes to crash them into important buildings, including the Twin Towers of the World Trade Center in New York City.
- Josephine Harris successfully escaped the North Tower with the help of New York City firefighters from Ladder Company 6.
- While escaping from the 84th floor of the South Tower, Brian Clark stopped to free Stanley Praimnath, who was trapped in rubble and crying for help. Both men escaped together and became close friends.
- Lauren Manning was burned on more than 80 percent of her body when a fireball hit her in the lobby of the North Tower. She underwent numerous surgeries and several years of physical therapy.
- After being trapped for more than 27 hours under the rubble of the collapsed North Tower, Genelle Guzman-McMillan was the final survivor pulled from the wreckage of the Twin Towers.

More than 6,000 people were injured in the September 11 attacks.

NYC

CHAPTER ONE

JOSEPHINE HARRIS AND LADDER COMPANY 6

On the morning of September 11, 2001, 59-year-old Josephine Harris went to work like any other day. She was a **bookkeeper** for the Port Authority. The Port Authority owns the World Trade Center, where Harris worked. It also works on transportation projects in New York and New Jersey.

In 2002, Josephine Harris (front left) reunited with (from left) Bill Butler, Matt Komorowski, Jay Jonas (front right), Mike Meldrum, and Sal D'Agostino to tell their story at the Fire Safety Learning Center.

Harris worked in the North Tower. Her office was on the 73rd floor. It should have been a normal Tuesday.

But at 8:46 a.m., the unthinkable happened. A plane hit the North Tower. Harris and many others felt the explosion and the rumbling of the tower. She knew they had to get out of the building. But the tower was 110 stories tall.

A few months earlier, Harris had suffered a leg injury. She was still limping as she began the long descent down Stairwell B. Smoke and dust filled the stairwell. The frightened people struggled to see as they moved down the stairs. Meanwhile, firefighters were trying to get up the stairs. Six men from Ladder Company 6 had reached the 27th floor. Jay Jonas was their captain. The others were Sal D'Agostino, Bill Butler, Tommy Falco, Matt Komorowski, and Mike Meldrum. They were trying to get to the 96th floor, where the plane had hit. Each firefighter was carrying 100 pounds (45 kg) of equipment to fight the fire. But just before 10 a.m., they heard a loud noise. The building swayed back and forth. Jonas learned that the South Tower had collapsed. He told his men they needed to **evacuate**. They started back down the stairs.

Harris struggled down 50 floors before she broke down in tears around the 20th floor. Exhausted and in pain, she could not make it any farther. That was when Ladder Company 6 reached Harris. A firefighter asked Jonas, "Cap, what do you want to do with her?" Other people had run past Harris. But Jonas would later say, "That's not in the culture of the Fire Department. . . . If somebody needs help, we got to give it a shot." The captain said they would bring Harris with them.

Butler was the strongest man on the crew. He put Harris's arm around his shoulder and began helping her down the stairs. The whole company slowed down to stay together. Jonas was worried they were going too slowly. Luckily, they were getting close to the exit. But around the fifth floor, Harris collapsed. She could not take another step. She told the firefighters to go on without her.

Meanwhile, Port Authority officer David Lim was coming down the stairs with Kathy Mazza, a Port Authority captain. She told Lim to keep moving, but he told her to go ahead. Lim and Butler began carrying Harris.

When the group arrived at the fourth floor, they heard a rumble. It was 10:28 a.m. The noise became incredibly loud. Then came the wind. The North Tower was collapsing. Each floor was crashing down onto the floor below. With each crash, a hurricane-like wind was forced down the stairwell.

Firefighters from all over New York City responded to the World Trade Center attacks.

The firefighters were blown off their feet. Komorowski was hurled from the fourth floor down to the second. The wind lifted him over Lim's head.

The collapse lasted around 10 seconds. Then the noise and the wind came to an abrupt stop. The stairwell was dark from smoke and dust. The firefighters began shouting to one another. Miraculously, all six members of Ladder Company 6 were alive. So were Lim and Harris. There were six other firefighters in the stairwell who survived, too. The tower had collapsed above and below Harris and the others. This small section of the stairwell was the only part of the tower that was spared. Captain Mazza did not make it out. Lim realized if he had not slowed down, he would have died, too. "Josephine Harris saved my life," he later said. Many of the firefighters felt the same way. A few weeks later, Harris reunited with her brave firefighters. The crew from Ladder Company 6 presented her with a jacket with the words *Guardian Angel* embroidered on it.

When Harris passed away in 2011, she was given a full firefighter's funeral. Members of Ladder Company 6 carried her coffin. The outside had a firefighter symbol and the words *Guardian Angel of 9/11*. The inside had an embroidered image of a firefighter walking hand-in-hand with an angel.

Most of the people inside the North Tower who survived its collapse were in the same section of Stairwell B as Ladder Company 6. ►

CHAPTER TWO

BRIAN CLARK AND STANLEY PRAIMNATH

Brian Clark arrived at work around 7:15 a.m. on September 11, 2001. His office was on the 84th floor of the South Tower. He was an executive vice president at Euro Brokers. This company helps people buy and sell stocks and other investments. At 8:46 a.m., he heard an enormous *thump*.

◄ **Many businesses with offices in the Twin Towers were financial companies.**

The lights overhead buzzed. Clark turned around to look out his office window. All he saw were flames.

Clark assumed there had been an explosion a floor or two above him. He was a designated fire marshal. Fire marshals help make sure people are prepared for emergency situations. Clark grabbed his whistle and flashlight. He shouted for people to get out and began leading people toward the exits.

Then Clark and his coworkers learned that there had been no explosion in their tower. TV news stories said a plane had hit the North Tower next door. Some people continued to rush to the stairs. Others stayed to watch the news. Clark called his wife, telling her to turn on the TV.

At 8:55 a.m., there was an announcement on the intercom system. It said the building was secure and people did not need to evacuate. Clark and his coworkers were relieved. But at 9:03 a.m., a second plane hit the South Tower. It plowed through floors 77 through 85. Around Clark and his colleagues, the ceiling fell apart, floor tiles buckled, and door frames popped out of the walls and fell.

With dust and **debris** thick in the air, Clark turned on his flashlight. He made his way to the center of the building.

He started down Stairway A with a few others. They made it down three floors when they met two people coming up from the 80th floor. They said there was too much fire to go down. They were making their way to the roof. They hoped a helicopter would come rescue them. As Clark's group stood in the stairway arguing over which way to go, they heard banging coming from the 81st floor. Someone was calling for help. Clark grabbed another man in the group, Ron DiFrancesco, and went looking for the person.

Clark and DiFrancesco pushed aside debris. "Can you see my hand?" a man yelled. Clark saw a hand sticking out from a hole in the wall. DiFrancesco was overcome with smoke and had to turn back. Clark went on alone. He moved the debris that was trapping the man. Clark pulled, the man jumped, and they fell backward in a heap together. Stanley Praimnath, an assistant vice president at Fuji Bank, was finally free.

Praimnath had been sitting at his desk on the 81st floor when he saw an airplane fly past the Statue of Liberty. The plane flew closer and closer. It crashed into the building only 130 feet (39.6 m) away from him. Just before the impact, Praimnath dove under his desk. His office burst into flames. Realizing that he was trapped, he began yelling for help.

Once Clark pulled Praimnath free, the two introduced themselves. "We'll be brothers for life," Praimnath said.

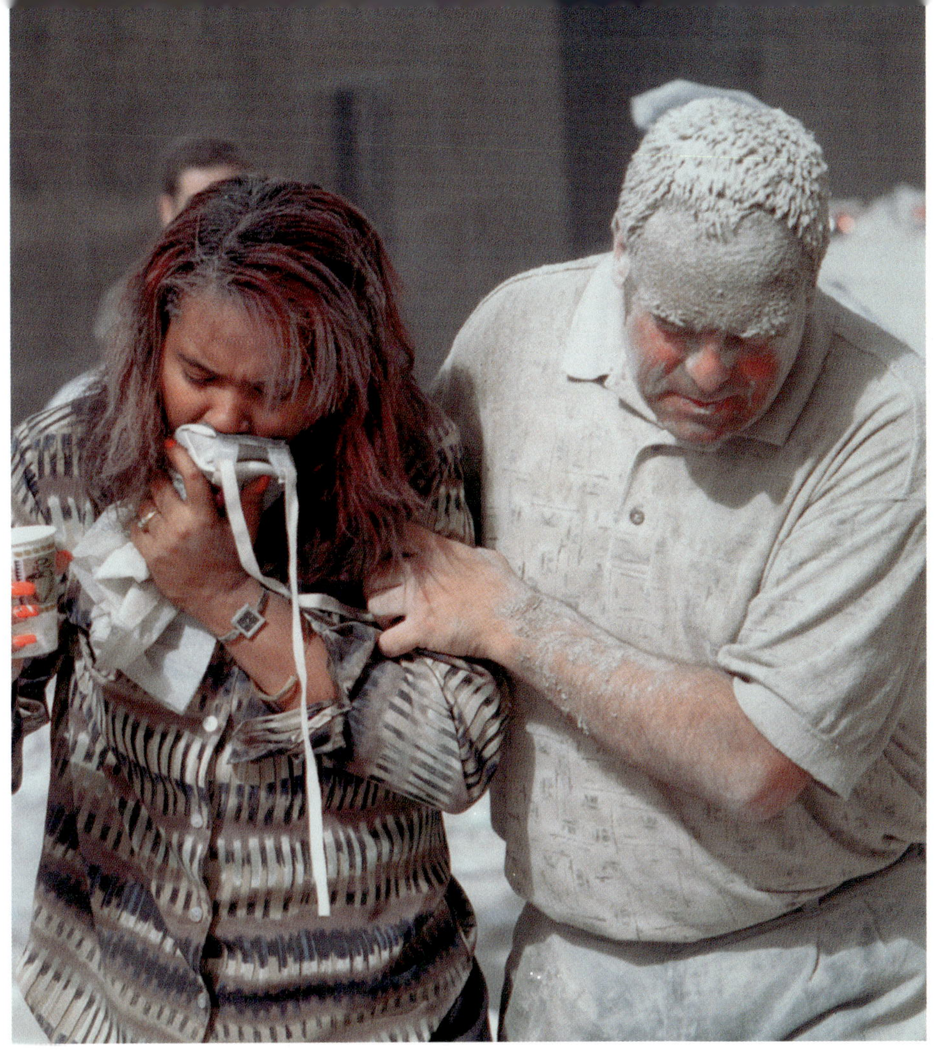

Many 9/11 survivors have developed health problems from the dust and debris in the air after the attacks.

Clark put his arm around Praimnath. "C'mon buddy," he said, "let's go home."

Praimnath and Clark returned to the stairway, but the others were not there. Clark assumed they had all gone back up the stairs. The two men decided to continue going down. For the first five floors, the men had to move a lot of debris out of their way.

But then the air got clearer. They were able to descend the stairs more quickly and easily.

They stopped on the 31st floor and went into an office. They each called their wives to reassure them they were okay. Then they continued their descent. Clear of the smoke and fire, the men were taking their time. Clark joked to Praimnath, "Hey, let's not go too fast here. I'd hate to break an ankle and have to walk 30 floors or something."

The two men reached the lobby of the tower. Everything was deserted. They were shocked when they caught a glimpse of the Plaza outside. "It was a moonscape," Clark said. "It looked like it had been deserted for 100 years, and we had just discovered it." The World Trade Center buildings were connected by a large underground area with a subway station, shopping mall, and more. The two men exited through 4 World Trade Center. They made their way toward Trinity Church, where they met two ministers.

Praimnath immediately broke down crying. "This man saved my life," he said. Clark became emotional as well. "You know, Stanley, you may think I saved your life, but I think you saved my life, too," he said. "You got me out of that argument as to whether I should go up or go down. . . . It's because of your voice in the darkness that I made it."

A 2011 exhibit featured portraits of Richard Fern, Stanley Praimnath, Brian Clark, and Ron DiFrancesco. These four men were the only people above the South Tower's impact site who survived. Clark (left) and Fern (right) are shown with the photos. DiFrancesco eventually came down the same staircase as Clark and Praimnath, becoming one of the last people to escape the South Tower.

Only four people in the floors above the South Tower crash site survived. Clark and Praimnath were two of them. They escaped just minutes before the building collapsed. Clark and Praimnath remained close friends in the years following 9/11. "We are bonded for life because of what we went through, and he's more than a friend. Brian is a big brother," Praimnath explained.

YEAR
GLAMOUR

CHAPTER THREE

LAUREN MANNING

Lauren Manning was a senior executive at Cantor Fitzgerald financial services. Their offices were on the 101st through 105th floors of the North Tower. At 8:46 a.m. on September 11, 2001, Manning was in the building's lobby. As she neared the elevators, she heard an ear-splitting sound. She thought it was construction.

More than 100 floors up, Manning's colleagues sat at their desks. They, too, had heard the noise and felt a small tremble in the building. Just below them, a plane had crashed into floors 93 through 99. The plane's fuel caught fire when it crashed. Manning's colleagues were trapped. Manning was standing in front of the elevator when the doors exploded open. She was engulfed in flames.

Senator Hillary Clinton (left) presented a *Glamour* Magazine Woman of the Year Award to Lauren Manning in 2002.

The 9/11 Memorial and Museum in New York City has an elevator motor from the World Trade Center wreckage on display.

Manning's quick thinking kicked into gear. As her back and arms ignited, she raced out of the lobby and across six lanes of traffic to a patch of grass. With the help of two strangers, she dropped to the ground and rolled until the flames were extinguished. Years later, Manning recalled, "I was in complete and utter pain, I knew I needed a burn center."

Manning was first taken to a hospital with no specialized burn unit. Ten hours later, she was transferred to a burn center.

There were 17 other burn victims with Manning. Only 12 of them survived. Burns covered more than 80 percent of Manning's body, and most were third-degree burns. Some areas had fourth- and fifth-degree burns. Manning's lungs had also been injured.

Doctors gave Manning medication to keep her unconscious. This is called a medically induced coma. Doctors do this when a person is severely injured to give the body time to heal.

BURN DEGREES

Degrees describe how bad a burn is. Lower-degree burns are less severe than high-degree burns.

First-degree burns affect only the outer layer of skin.

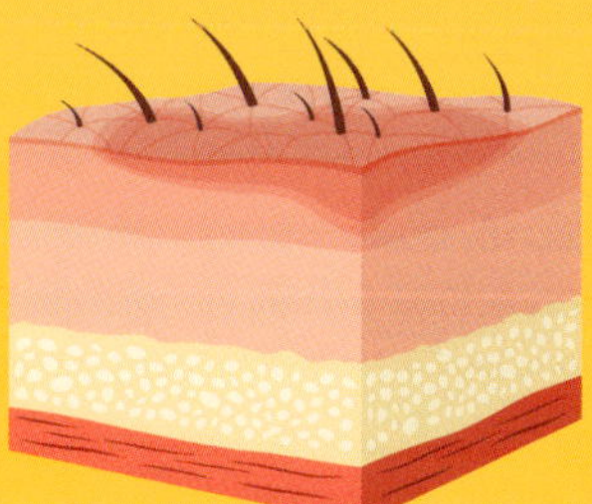

Second-degree burns affect the outer layer and part of the next layer of skin.

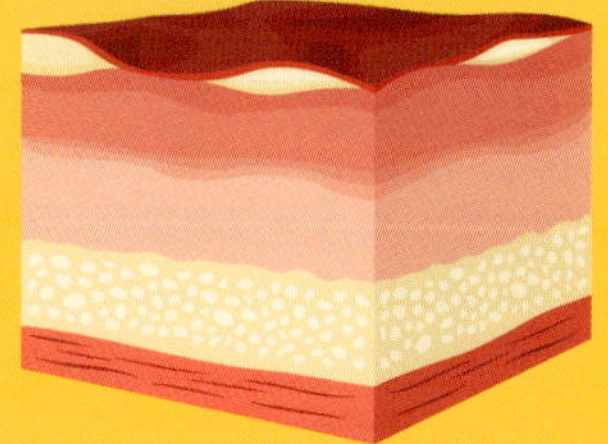

Third-degree burns destroy the outer layer of skin and the layer underneath.

Fourth- and fifth-degree burns can reach muscles or bones.

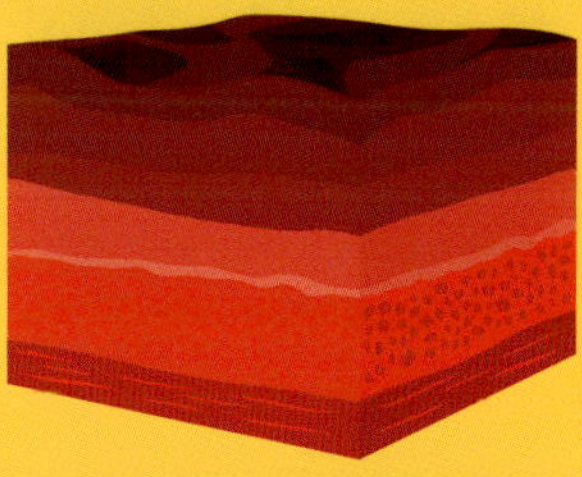

Lauren Manning, pictured in 2016, co-founded a company that works with consumer privacy.

Manning remained in a coma for nearly two months. She went through 11 surgeries. Some of her badly burned fingers had to be **amputated**. Doctors used **skin grafts** to heal Manning's burned skin. Manning also fought off severe infections.

When she awoke, Manning had a long road to recovery. She worked with physical and occupational therapists. These therapists help people recover after an injury. The process was excruciatingly painful. But Manning pushed through. She wanted to return home to her son, Tyler. He had just turned one. Three days after walking only 4 feet (1.2 m) before nearly passing out, Manning made it 30 feet (9.1 m) to the nurses' station. Therapists, doctors, nurses, and her parents cheered her on. Manning explained, "I felt an incredible surge of freedom. Everyone was clapping and crying, and I realized that my fight was their fight and that we were a team."

Manning was released from the hospital after 91 days and went to a **rehabilitation** center. Finally, in March 2002, she was able to return home. She continued to have surgeries to help her recovery. Ten years after the attacks, Manning published a book about her experience. She became a motivational speaker.

Manning lost 658 coworkers at Cantor Fitzgerald on 9/11. She says not a day goes by that she doesn't think of those who were not given a second chance like she was. "Before the attacks, I used to breeze right by the little things, all those expected or mundane activities that you don't pay attention to, like seeing a friend for lunch or bringing your son to school," she said. "I treasure each of these simple and joyful moments now."

CHAPTER FOUR

GENELLE GUZMAN-McMILLAN

Genelle Guzman-McMillan was born and grew up in Trinidad and Tobago, an island off the coast of Venezuela. She moved to the United States in the late 1990s. By 2001, she was working as an office administrative assistant with the Port Authority of New York and New Jersey.

◄ **In September 2021, Genelle Guzman-McMillan spoke about her 9/11 experience in Fort McCoy, Wisconsin.**

On September 11, 2001, Guzman-McMillan arrived at work. She went to her office on the 64th floor of the North Tower. The 31-year-old was chatting with her coworker and friend, Rosa Gonzalez. Suddenly, the two women felt the building shake. They ran to the window and noticed paper and debris falling from the sky. "I just thought something had blown up, up above," she said. "I heard noise, but the shake was what was scary. It was like an earthquake or something. I had no clue what was going on."

Guzman-McMillan learned that a plane had hit the building. News broadcasts on televisions in the office said it was a terrorist attack. She felt the building shake again. She and Gonzalez knew they had to evacuate. They hurried to a staircase and started down the 64 floors, holding hands.

When they arrived at the 13th floor, Guzman-McMillan stopped briefly to remove her high heels. "I really thought we were almost there," she recalled. But in that instant, the tower began to sway. "The floor buckled. Pieces of the walls and ceiling rained down. Dust was everywhere," Guzman-McMillan said. "I fell down flat on my face. In a flash, the deafening rumble gave way to silence as eerie and terrible in its own way as the roar had been. . . . I was alive. Was anyone else?"

TOWER MAP

Each of the Twin Towers was 110 stories tall.

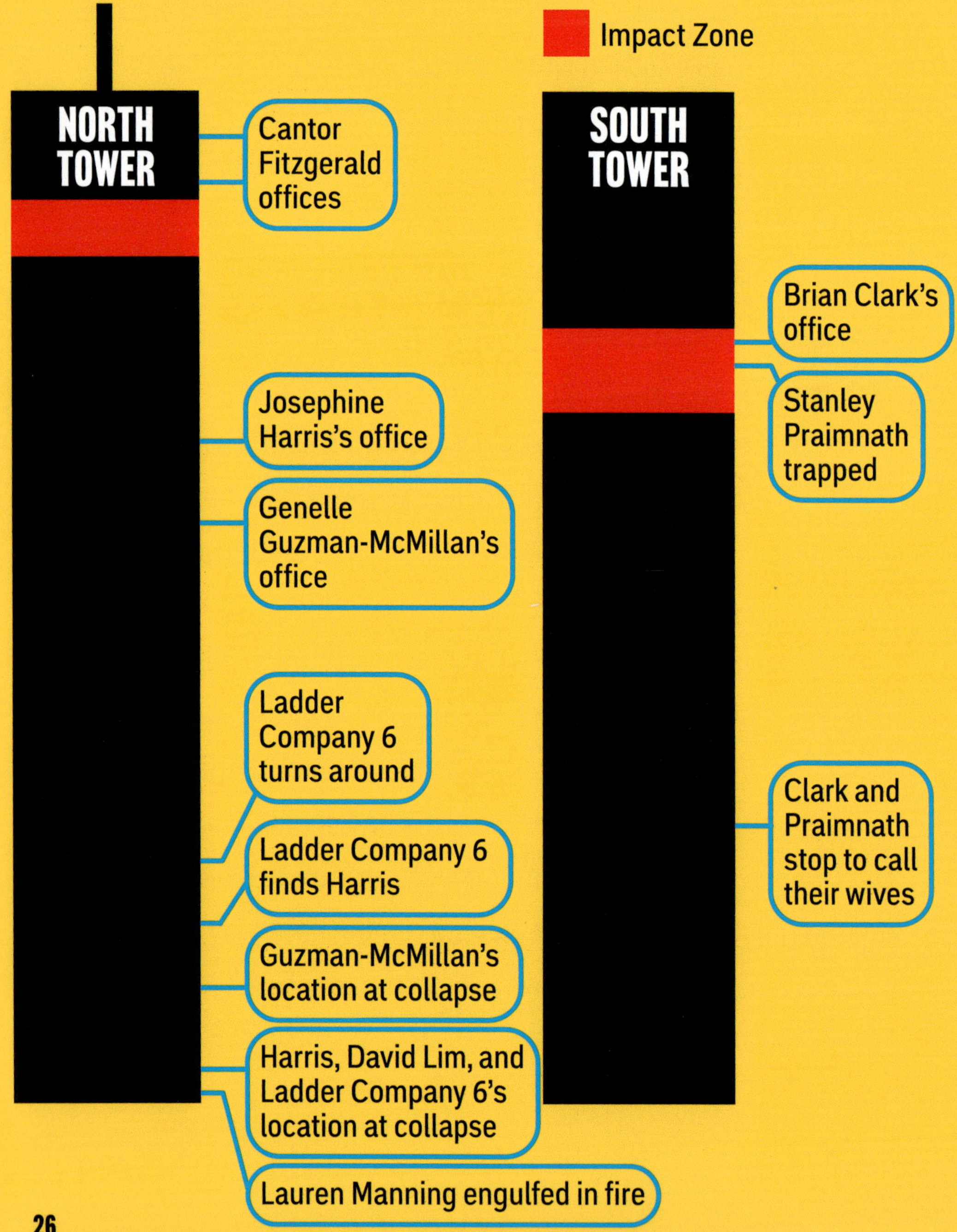

Rescue workers began calling the remains of the World Trade Center "the Pile."

Guzman-McMillan was trapped. Her leg was buried in debris. Her head was stuck between two pillars. She laid there for 27 hours, in pain and drifting in and out of sleep. "I decided to pray," she said. "I just kept begging and praying, just asking God to show me a miracle."

Just as she started to give up hope, she heard a voice. Someone was nearby! She called for help, clawing through debris with her left hand. Someone grabbed it. "Don't worry," a man's voice said. "My name is Paul. Just hang on. They're going to get you out of there." Rescue workers worked for more than an hour.

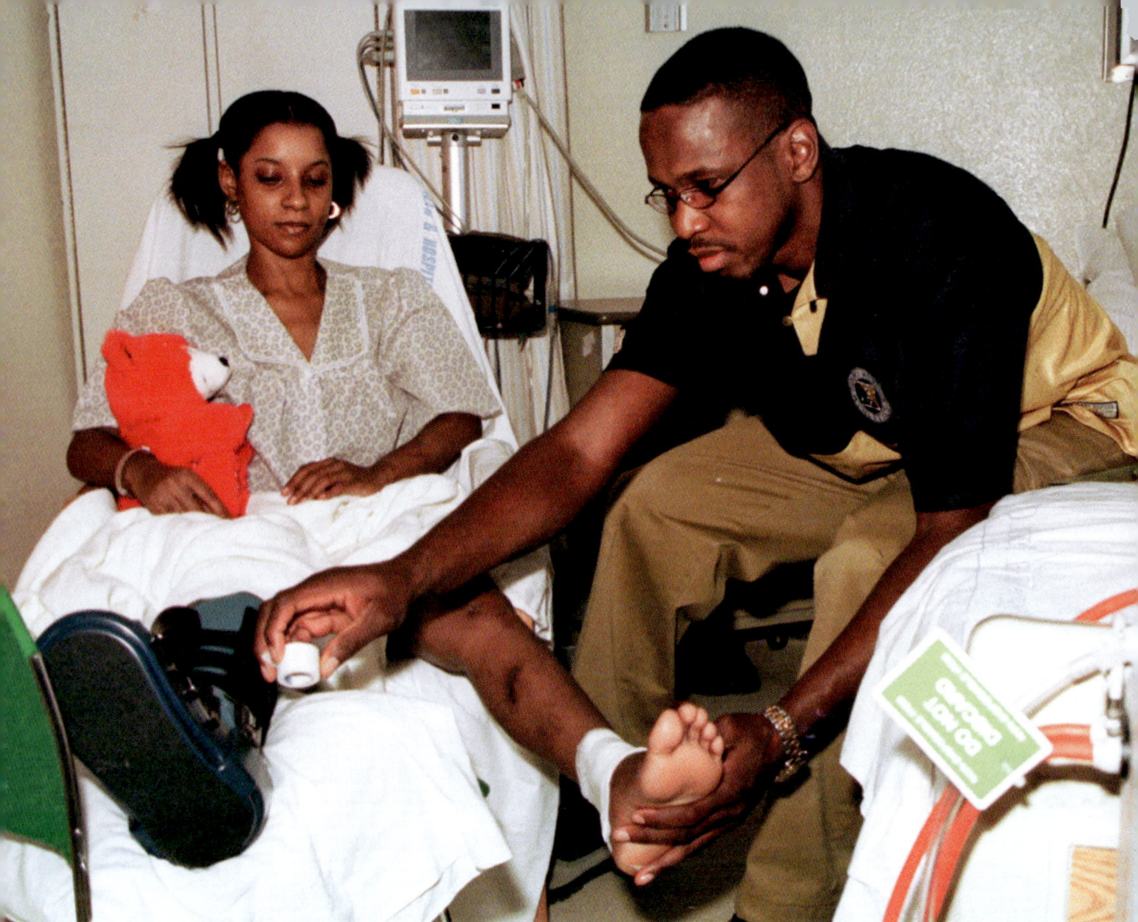

The week Genelle Guzman (left) was released from the hospital, she married her then boyfriend, Roger McMillan (right).

They finally managed to pull her from the rubble. They placed her on a stretcher and passed her down a line of people toward the street. At the bottom of the path, Guzman-McMillan heard people cheering. She proved to be the final survivor pulled from the wreckage.

Guzman-McMillan had serious injuries. Doctors thought her leg might need to be amputated. But after six weeks in the hospital and four surgeries, Guzman-McMillan was released.

She searched for Paul after her rescue. But no one knew who he was. She became convinced he had been her guardian angel. Ten years later, Guzman-McMillan published a book about her experience. Afterward, she and her coauthor heard from firefighters who had been there that day. One of them was Paul Somin. He was the Paul who had held her hand. Guzman-McMillan was not certain that this was her Paul. But as one reader told her co-author, "It really doesn't matter whether he was an angel from above or if he was human. I believe he was still sent to her by God, and he will always be her angel."

THINK ABOUT IT

- Ladder Company 6 stopped to help Josephine Harris, and Brian Clark rescued Stanley Praimnath. These actions could have prevented them from escaping, but they ultimately saved their lives. What would you have done in their situation? Why?
- Lauren Manning and Genelle Guzman-McMillan both suffered major injuries. Read the stories about each of their recoveries again. What do they have in common?
- What are steps you can take to be prepared in an emergency?
- Some of these survivors did not evacuate right away. Why do you think that is?

GLOSSARY

amputated (AMP-yoo-tay-ted): When a body part is amputated, it is cut off because it is no longer healthy. Some of Lauren Manning's burned fingers were amputated.

bookkeeper (BOOK-kee-pur): A bookkeeper keeps track of a business's expenses and income. Josephine Harris worked as a bookkeeper for the Port Authority.

debris (duh-BREE): Debris is made up of pieces of things that have been destroyed or broken down. Stanley Praimnath was trapped by debris until Brian Clark helped him get free.

evacuate (eh-VAK-yoo-ayt): To evacuate means to leave a place where one might be in danger. Some people did not evacuate the Twin Towers right away.

hijacked (HY-jakt): When something has been hijacked, it has been taken over by force. Terrorists hijacked airplanes on September 11, 2001.

rehabilitation (ree-huh-bill-uh-TAY-shun): Rehabilitation is therapy that restores health, function, or movement after an illness or injury. Lauren Manning went to a special rehabilitation center after being released from the hospital.

skin grafts (SKIN GRAFTZ): Skin grafts are medical treatments in which healthy skin is placed over damaged or burned areas of the body. Lauren Manning needed skin grafts for her burns.

terrorists (TAYR-ur-ists): Terrorists are people who commit violent acts to make people feel fear or terror. Terrorists were behind the September 11 attacks.

SELECTED BIBLIOGRAPHY

Carter, Chelsea J. "Faces of 9/11: Where Are They Now?" *CNN*, 11 Sept. 2014. www.cnn.com. Accessed 20 Dec. 2023.

Herbst, Diane. "9/11: The Last Person Pulled Out Alive from World Trade Center Rubble: 'I Was Given a New Life.'" *People*, 11 Sept. 2021. people.com. Accessed 20 Dec. 2023.

NYP News. "Amazing Things: Lauren Manning." *NewYork-Presbyterian Health Matters*, n.d., healthmatters.nyp.org. Accessed 20 Dec. 2023.

FIND OUT MORE

BOOKS

Huddleston, Emma. *Looking Inside the Human Body*. Parker, CO: The Child's World, 2020.

Rea, Amy C. *Rescue Dogs on 9/11*. Parker, CO: The Child's World, 2025.

Romero, Libby. *September 11*. Washington, DC: National Geographic Kids, 2021.

WEBSITES

Visit our website for links about survivors on 9/11:
childsworld.com/links

Note to Parents, Caregivers, Teachers, and Librarians: We routinely verify our web links to make sure they are safe and active sites. So encourage your readers to check them out!

INDEX